A MEDITATION ON I AM

A MEDITATION ON

I Am

Rupert Spira

SAHAJA

newharbinger
publications

SAHAJA PUBLICATIONS

PO Box 887, Oxford OX1 9PR
www.sahajapublications.com

A co-publication with New Harbinger Publications
5674 Shattuck Avenue, Oakland, CA 94609
United States of America

Distributed in Canada by Raincoast Books

Designed by Rob Bowden

Printed in the United States of America on 100% recycled paper

ISBN 978-1-68403-794-0

Library of Congress Cataloging-in-Publication Data
on file with publisher

Turn towards Me
and I will take you into Myself

THE UNITY OF BEING

T hroughout our lives we make statements such as, 'I am five years old', 'I am twenty-four years old', 'I am lonely', 'I am in love', 'I am excited', 'I am depressed', 'I am having lunch', 'I am reading a book', 'I am married', 'I am single', and so on.

In each of these statements we refer to our basic self or being – 'I am' – which is subsequently coloured by various thoughts, feelings, states of mind, activities or relationships. In each of these descriptions a temporary quality or characteristic is added to our being and, as a result, 'I am' becomes, or seems to become, 'I am this or that'.

The contents of experience are continuously changing. No thought, feeling, state of mind, activity or relationship is essential to us. They seem to temporarily qualify our self, but our basic sense of being remains the same throughout. It is the changeless background of our ever-changing experience.

We are now the same self that we were yesterday, that we were last year and that we were as a young child. The self who experiences loneliness or depression is the same self who knows excitement or the experience of being in love, just as the one who was in a relationship is the same one who is now single.

What accounts for this conviction that we are always the same person? After all, none of our thoughts, images, feelings, sensations, perceptions, activities or relationships remain the same. And yet there is undoubtedly a current that runs consistently throughout all changing experience.

* * *

Our being or self is the constant factor in all changing experience, just as a screen is the stable background upon which all movies are played. In a movie, no two images appear concurrently; if they did, they would be the same image. Therefore, no single image is directly related to any other in the film.

It is the screen that lends continuity to this otherwise discontinuous set of images, allowing the movie to appear as an undivided whole rather than a series of fragmented parts. Likewise, our being lends its ever-presence to the ever-changing flow of objective experience, conferring unity and continuity upon it.

Our being is not itself an experience but enables all experience to occur, just as the screen permits a film to be played. There could be no experience without our self, just as there can be no movie without a screen.

Our self is the common thread that weaves the tapestry of life into a coherent whole, the ever-present fibre that unites what would otherwise be a fragmented patchwork of thoughts, images, feelings, sensations and perceptions. It is the luminous thread that confers integrity and

4

coherence upon our ever-changing experience, thereby accounting for the undeniable unity and continuity of experience.

The screen is the colourless background of all the coloured images in a film. As such, it shares none of the limitations that characterise the objects, people or events in the movie. At the same time, the screen is not separate from the film; it pervades each and every scene. Each image, after all, is simply a temporary modulation of the screen.

Similarly, our self shares none of the limits that characterise the content of experience, that is, our thoughts, images, feelings, sensations, perceptions, activities and relationships. Our being is the objectless, aware presence that lies behind and, at the same time, intimately pervades all experience.

As such, our being both transcends the limitations of experience and is immanent within them.

* * *

Divested of the qualities that it borrows from experience, our essential nature is unlimited or infinite. As such, our being is not 'our' being; it is simply *being*. Just as the screen is not a property of any particular image or movie, so being is not a property of any particular object or person. It is simply the intimate, impersonal, infinite being from which everyone and everything derives its apparently independent existence.

In relation to ourself, our shared being is referred to as 'I'. In relation to the universe, it is sometimes referred to as 'God'.

Although both these words have associations and, therefore, limitations, each conveys something of the nature of the reality to which it refers. The word 'I' denotes the intimacy of our shared being, while the word 'God' evokes its impersonal, infinite nature. We might simply refer to it as 'presence', because presence is the common factor in all that is.

Given that we are inextricably linked to the universe, our essential nature and that of the cosmos must be one and the same, just as the nature of a wave and the nature of the ocean are one. This understanding was expressed by Jesus when he said, 'I and my Father are one'. That is, my essential being and the being of the universe are one.

The same understanding is expressed in Buddhism, 'Nirvana and samsara are one', indicating that the essential nature of our mind and the reality of the world are the same. This universal truth is echoed in the Hindu religion, 'Atman and Brahman are identical'. That is, the apparently individual being of every person is God's universal being.

In the Sufi tradition, 'Whosoever knows their self knows their Lord', that is, whosoever knows what is designated by the name 'I' or 'I am' stands identified with the ultimate reality of the universe. In other words, the ultimate reality shines in each of our minds as the knowledge 'I' or 'I am', before it is coloured or qualified by experience. As such, 'I am' is the divine name.

* * *

There can be no endeavour of greater importance than the journey to know oneself: to recognise one's essential nature, that which gives birth to existence. Indeed, if we do not know the nature of being, how could we know the nature of anything that exists?

The word 'existence' is derived from two Latin words, *ex-*, meaning 'out of' or 'from', and *sistere*, meaning 'to stand'. This implies that anything that exists *stands out from* the background of being, just as the objects and people in a movie stand out from the background of a screen. Of course, no object or person in a film actually stands apart from the screen; they only seem to. Likewise, no object or person stands apart from the background of pure being; they only seem to.

This understanding is echoed in the Bhagavad Gita, 'That which is never ceases to be; that which is not never comes into existence'. And in the Muslim tradition it is said, *'La ilaha illallah'*, meaning, 'There is no God but God', that is, no person is a self unto their self and no thing is a thing unto itself.

Nothing has its own existence, but rather everything borrows its apparent existence from God's being, the only being there is. There is only one reality, and that reality stands alone, indivisible, indestructible, whole, perfect and complete.

Just as all movies are a colouring of a single, indivisible screen, so all people and things are a modulation of pure being. Being is 'pure' because there is nothing in being other than being itself with which it could be mixed or limited. As such, it is infinite, indivisible and, at the same time, utterly intimate. It shines in our self as the knowledge 'I' or 'I am'.

This does not imply any disparagement of people or things. On the contrary, we are elevating people and things to their proper status. We are relieving the world of its status as an object to be exploited, and we are liberating people from the projection of 'other' to be oppressed, thus alleviating both from the inevitable consequences that attend such beliefs.

In other words, we are removing the filter of beliefs through which the universe has been fragmented into an apparent multiplicity of objects and others. We are discerning the unity of being in the diversity of existence, the 'white radiance of eternity' in the 'dome of many-coloured glass', as the poet Shelley put it. In the filmmaker Pasolini's words, we are 'restoring to reality its original sacred significance'.

*   *   *

When the unity of being shines in our relationship with another person, we experience it as love. Our being recognises itself in the apparent other. As the Sufi mystic Balyani said, 'Otherness for Him is Him without otherness'. It is for this reason that Rumi said, 'True lovers never really meet; they are in each other all along'.

And when our experience of an object – such as a painting, sculpture, bowl, dance, piece of music or landscape – momentarily dissolves the subject–object relationship through which we normally perceive, we experience the revelation of beauty. As with the experience of love, in which the separation between ourself and the apparent other dissolves, so in the experience of beauty, the distinction between ourself and the object or world subsides.

As such, love and beauty are revelations of reality, the shining of being in the midst of the apparent multiplicity and diversity of objects and selves. They are the revelation of God's presence, which shines as the am-ness in all selves and the is-ness in all things.

Ultimately, our being cannot legitimately be given a name, for all names have evolved to describe the content of experience. Even to call being 'infinite' is to say too much, as this suggests that there could be something real in existence that is finite, with which it could be contrasted. That would give credence to the idea that there is something other than God's being, and that is blasphemy.

Even the name 'being' goes too far, as it implies its opposite, non-being. If we wish to speak of being, we should really remain silent. As the painter Chatin Sarachi once said to my mother, 'If God exists, how do you dare even mention his name?'

And yet, paradoxically, how could anything be more worthy of our interest, love and attention than that from which all objects and selves derive their apparently independent existence? It is that which can never be captured in words, and yet all words speak only of it. It is that which can never be portrayed by art, and yet all art issues forth in its service. It is that which demands our silence, and yet all speech – and all poetry – pours out in its name.

As a Zen master once said, 'If I speak, I tell a lie; if I remain silent, I am a coward'. It is in this spirit that, over a number of years, the words of this poem took shape in my mind.

Rupert Spira
OXFORD, MAY 2020

I AM

I am

I have no words to express Myself
but all words express only Me

I have no meaning
but impart meaning to all that is perceived

I am without beginning and end
but all things begin and end in Me

I have no name
but am called by all names

I have no form
but all form indicates Me

I have no origin
but am the origin of all things

I am without division
but all divisions exist in Me

I am the knowing with which all things
are known

I am the presence in which all things appear

I am the substance out of which all things
are made

I am and know Myself alone

I shine in the mind as the knowledge 'I am'

I pervade the body as the feeling of being

I am felt in the heart as peace and happiness

It is My being that shines as existence in all things

I am the longing in sadness
and the longed for in all longing

I am the expecting
and the expected in all expectation

I am the restlessness of the restless

I am the peace of the peaceful

I am happiness itself

I cannot be contemplated
but am the object of all contemplation

I am imperceivable
yet you perceive only Me

I am full but have nothing

I am empty but contain all

I give away everything
but am never diminished

I receive all but never expand

I am everyone's lover

I shine

I speak but am silent

I move whilst at rest

I know but cannot be known

I experience but cannot be experienced

I am but do not exist

I think but cannot be thought about

I feel but cannot be felt

I see but cannot be seen

I hear but cannot be heard

I touch but cannot be touched

I taste but cannot be tasted

I smell but cannot be smelt

I smile

Whatever appears, appears in Me
but I do not appear

I am the silence in music
and the music in silence

I am concealed in the world
but reveal the world

I am the womb and the tomb
of all that exists

I offer and contain in one gesture
like an open bowl

I give Myself unconditionally to all things

I embrace all others but know no otherness

I receive all things without choice

I am the knowing in all that is known

I am the experiencing in all that is
experienced

I am the allowing of all things

I am empty of objects but full of Myself

I am open without resistance

I am eclipsed by you
but you are illumined by Me

I am the sun in the moon

I am the friendship of friends

I am knowing and unknowing

I am dark in the day and bright at night

I am luminous

All colours borrow their light
from My luminosity

All lovers borrow their affection
from My love

All things borrow their existence
from My being

All knowledge is a reflection
of My intelligence

I am inexhaustible

I am yours and mine

I am the yes in the no

I am the now in the then

I am the here in the there

I am the me in the you

I am the this in the that

I am the always in the never

I am the uncertainty of all things
and the certainty of uncertainty

I am the security of insecurity

I am the true in the false

I am the dignity in pride

I am the reality of an illusion

I am the existence of all that exists

I move but am motionless
am motionless but move

I am concealed in boredom
but am not Myself boring

I am veiled by doubt
but am not Myself in doubt

I live beneath fear
but am neither afraid nor frightening

I abide in Myself

If you look in front I am behind

If you look behind I am in front

If you look above I am below

If you look below I am above

I am hidden but never obscured

I am obvious but cannot be found

I am the bright, self-luminous emptiness
of the mirror

And the colourful, dancing images
that appear in it

It is from Me that the world borrows
its reality

I am immanent and transcendent

I break open the body
and spread it across the world

I break open the world
and hold it dismembered in My heart

I am pregnant with the universe

I am the unknown in the known
and the known in the unknown

I am the love in hatred
and the hope in despair

I am the same in all difference
and different in the same

I am the isness of things
and the amness of self

I cannot be approached
but am always present

I cannot be known
but know all things

I cannot be understood
but am all that is ever known

I do not exist but am never absent

I am nowhere and everywhere

I am nothing and everything

I play

Whenever you think of Me
it is I who am thinking of you

Whenever you love Me
it is I who am loving you

Whenever you long for Me
it is I who am longing for you

Your desire for happiness
is the pull of My grace in your heart

I am the knowledge in ignorance

I am the answer in the question

I give Myself and receive Myself perpetually

I lend Myself to all seeming things

The universe is My activity

I forget Myself
for the sweetness of longing

I divide Myself
for the tenderness of friendship

I hide Myself
for the pleasure of seeking

I look for Myself
for the fulfilment of finding

I find Myself
for the knowledge of happiness

I know Myself for the joy of being

I am Myself for no other reason

I become ugly for the sake of beauty

I become hostile for the sake of love

I become cruel for the sake of kindness

I am vast and bright

I am the heart of the heart

I am the voice of a child

I am wonder, astonishment and delight

I live in the space between thoughts
but I play in your thinking

My abode is the moment between breaths
but I dance in your breathing

Time and space move through Me
but I do not move through them

I am self-aware, self-luminous
and self-evident

I am never experienced
yet you experience only Me

I never repeat Myself
but am always the same

I cannot be known
but am never not known

I am utterly vulnerable
but cannot be harmed

I am made of nothing
but cannot be destroyed

I have no defences
but am your refuge

I have no goal
but am the fulfilment of every desire

I have no feelings
but am open to all feelings

I have no thoughts
but all thoughts are images of Me

I am kindness itself

In ignorance I come and go in the world

In wisdom the world comes and goes in Me

In love the world is consumed in Me

I alone am

I am the relationship in all relationships

I am the understanding in all meaning

I am the permanent in all impermanence

It is My ever-presence that gives continuity
to time

It is My infinity that appears endless
in space

It is with My light that the world shines

I am lost in the world
and the world is lost in Me .

I am abundant yet empty
empty yet overflow

I am homeless at home everywhere

I am helpless but help all things

I have no cares but I care

I have no desires but I long for your heart

I wait without waiting

I render all experience knowable
but am not Myself an experience

I cannot be recognised
but recognise Myself in all things

I have no substance
but am the substance of all things

I have no experience
but am all experience

I depend on nothing
but all things depend on Me

I can never be found
but have never been lost

I am the embrace of lovers
and the love in an embrace

I am your call and you are My echo

I sing

I was not born but all are born of Me

I do not die but all things die in Me

I have no cause but cause all things

I do not last in time but all time lasts in Me

I am ordinary but extraordinary

I am the present in the past

I am the mirror of Narcissus

I am youthful but not young

I am ancient but not old

I am a fool but not foolish

I am a child but not childish

I am alone but not lonely

Whatever is seen I am seeing Myself

Whatever is heard I am hearing Myself

Whatever is touched I am touching Myself

Whatever is tasted I am tasting Myself

Whatever is smelt I am smelling Myself

Whatever is thought I am pondering Myself

Whatever is felt I am feeling Myself

Whatever is experienced in any way

I am always only experiencing Myself

I am not something but not nothing

I am not somewhere but not nowhere

I am not me but am not other

I am neither before nor after

I am neither beyond nor within

I do not exist but am not non-existent

I am desired and yet feared

I am longed for but avoided

How strange

I am closer than your breath
but further than the stars

I am vaster than space but have no size

I assume the shape of all things
but have no shape of My own

I know only Myself
and thus know no ignorance

I take the shape of thinking
and seem to become a mind

I assume the activity of sensing
and seem to become a body

I take the form of perceiving
and seem to become a world

But I always remain Myself

I am the self in all selves

I am the being in all that exists

I am intimate but impersonal

I am infinite and eternal

All things are known by Myself, in Myself,
as Myself

It is My being that is revealed as peace
when names and forms are dissolved in Me

It is My presence that is unveiled
as happiness whenever a desire is fulfilled

It is I who am felt as love in friendship

I am peace itself

I am emptiness vibrating
as the fullness of experience

I am fullness knowing itself
in the mirror of emptiness

I take the shape of all things without ever
becoming anything other than Myself

I am knowing, knowing only knowing

I am the love with which I am loved

I am the desire with which I am longed for

I am nothing but take the shape of
everything

I am nowhere but available everywhere

I hold on to nothing and cannot be held

All experience is a colouring of My being
but I have no colour of My own

I am concealed in the obvious
and obvious in the concealed

I am a mystery but am not mysterious

I am intimate with all things
but independent of all things

I am free

I clothe Myself in experience
veiling Myself with Myself

I divest Myself of experience
revealing Myself to Myself

I know no others
and am thus love itself

I know no objects
and am thus beauty itself

I am all that is known
and am thus truth itself

I am bound by nothing
and am thus freedom itself

I cannot be disturbed
and am thus peace itself

I know no lack
and am thus happiness itself

When the mind is present
I am known as thinking

When it dissolves in Me
I am known as understanding

When the body is present
I am known as feeling

When it melts into Me
I am known as happiness

When the world is present
I am known as perceiving

When it vanishes in Me
I am experienced as beauty

In the presence of others
I appear as relationship

When relationship dissolves
I shine as love

I have no meaning
but am the meaning of all that occurs

I have no purpose
but am that towards which everything tends

I am the origin, the substance and the
destiny of all things

I become something, then nothing,
then everything but always remain Myself

I can be separated from all things
but no thing can be separated from Me

I am in love with all that exists
and all that exists seeks Me alone

I live in eternity but dance in time

The world is My mirror and I am its lover

I am peaceful like the sky

I am open like the sea

I am empty like space

I am luminous like the sun

I shine by Myself

I am the light of pure knowing

Turn towards Me
and I will take you into Myself

I play

I enjoy

I am

BOWLS OUT OF WORDS

I wrote 'I Am' in the late 1990s and it has continued to develop in the intervening years. At that time I was working as a potter, throwing large, open bowls on the wheel, often engraving them with fine lines, which subsequently evolved into words, culminating in this poem.

Over the years, the bowls became larger, more open and increasingly delicate, often collapsing as the medium was stretched to its limit. Such a crack or breakdown of a structure, be it physical, psychological, social or cultural, often reveals that the content has outgrown its form, precipitating both a crisis and an opportunity.

At the time, the continued collapse of these pieces felt more like a failure than an invitation. However, one day, while engraving the poem 'I Am' onto a large, open bowl, whose precarious form threatened to disintegrate with every incision, the thought came to me, 'I'd like to make bowls just out of words'.

It was one of those thoughts that appear unsolicited, when the mind is relaxed and unfocused. Such a thought is not simply an extension of the past. It is an intervention, like a dream, revealing knowledge from the depths of one's being, knowledge that is often obscured by the clamour of the waking state.

I did not understand then what it might mean to 'make bowls out of words', and yet I knew the idea was significant. For a while it kept visiting me like the fading image of a dream, until in time it vanished. However, strangely and, of course, not so strangely, a couple of years later I found myself writing and speaking about the non-dual understanding, without ever having had the explicit intention of doing so.

It wasn't until someone specifically asked me about the transition from making bowls to speaking about these matters that I recalled that initial, unsolicited thought and realised that it had been a foretaste of what was to come. The medium has changed and I am, indeed, making bowls out of words.

PUBLICATIONS BY RUPERT SPIRA

The Transparency of Things
Contemplating the Nature of Experience
Non-Duality Press 2008,
Sahaja Publications & New Harbinger Publications 2016

Presence, Volume I
The Art of Peace and Happiness
Non-Duality Press 2011,
Sahaja Publications & New Harbinger Publications 2016

Presence, Volume II
The Intimacy of All Experience
Non-Duality Press 2011,
Sahaja Publications & New Harbinger Publications 2016

The Ashes of Love
Sayings on the Essence of Non-Duality
Non-Duality Press 2013, Sahaja Publications 2016

The Light of Pure Knowing
Thirty Meditations on the Essence of Non-Duality
Sahaja Publications 2014

Transparent Body, Luminous World
The Tantric Yoga of Sensation and Perception
Sahaja Publications 2016

The Nature of Consciousness
Essays on the Unity of Mind and Matter
Sahaja Publications & New Harbinger Publications 2017

Being Aware of Being Aware
The Essence of Meditation Series, Volume I
Sahaja Publications & New Harbinger Publications 2017

From an early age, Rupert Spira was deeply interested in the nature of reality and the source of lasting peace and happiness. He began to meditate at the age of seventeen and spent the next twenty years immersed in the teachings of classical Advaita Vedanta. In 1997 he met his teacher, Francis Lucille, who introduced him to the Direct Path approach of Atmananda Krishna Menon and the Tantric tradition of Kashmir Shaivism. More importantly, he indicated the means whereby one may recognise the source of lasting peace and happiness in oneself. Rupert lives in the United Kingdom. He has written several books and holds regular meetings and retreats online, as well as in Europe and the United States.

www.rupertspira.com